To Diane
Best Wishes!

Folks,
Will You Please Be Seated

D.W. Pettee

D.W. Pettee, Sr.

PublishAmerica
Baltimore

First printing

ISBN: 1-59129-747-8
PUBLISHED BY PUBLISHAMERICA BOOK
PUBLISHERS
www.publishamerica.com
Baltimore

Printed in the United States of America

Thanks to everyone who had a hand in the completion of this book in some way, shape, or form. This includes Dr. Dan Merritt; Dr. Steven Habusta; my three sons, David, Daniel, and Andrew; my parents, Francis and Dorothy Pettee; and above all, my loving wife and spirited partner, Jeannine, who has been a source of inspiration and unfaltering faith.

Preface:

"I am a teacher and I care about each and every one of you."
The student replied, "You are different."

Folks, there is no immediate solution to the challenges facing education today—no format, no single reform will change our direction until careful collaboration and consideration is given to the real-life challenges we face today. We must embrace solid statistical data on a timely basis so that we do not fall into the footprints of the past. You must believe that with every challenge we face today there is a positive solution; that finger-pointing is a waste of time, energy and talent. Ultimately, education must form a true partnership with industry and look at how we can come up with regional guidelines or standards that are universal. Then education can allow each state to carefully devise a method or application to achieve these standards. What are the variables? Cultural/Regional: allowing each community to keep its identity. Financial/Family: there are many variables that need careful consideration. That means the method we implement to achieve these goals may and will be different. What if the procedure by which we convey knowledge differs from state to state? In my opinion the knowledge learned or the skills developed will have universal success and ultimately help folks achieve a fulfilling life as well as becoming a contributing member of society. Let's factor in the variables so that the message sent is realized for its true meaning.

Chapter I:
First Encounter with Life and Consequences

Shouldn't our first encounter with life be one of love and the security of the family? Remember, family should be based on unconditional regard. If it is not, I believe this situation can be a major factor in living a fulfilling life ultimately to its highest level. Look at gangs: are they providing a sense of belonging? Are our young folks happy? I think we all know the sad results. So would you rather a gang provided your child security in his/ her early stages? Is your child a priority in life? If not, what are you doing to prepare them for life? Does the child ask the question, "Can I measure up?" What does the child do with this real or imagined unbearable sense of not measuring up? Could this lack of self-esteem and unhealthy respect for life lead to bodily harm, or worse yet, possibly suicide?

Question: What is the first organized structure that a child is an integral part of? It is the family. I am not sold on the fact that a child coming from a challenging early childhood can merely shrug off a way of life without appropriate counseling and direction in a formal educational setting. If there is a breakdown in the family structure, I believe it ultimately affects the perceived self-worth of the student. Could this send a message to the student that he or she cannot compete or do anything to succeed? Can fear of failure and fear of not measuring up complicated by low self-esteem and tremendous emotion prevent success and happiness? I believe it does. Given this thought I believe you must take an active interest in your loved ones. Keep in mind it could be quality of time enhanced with respect and love that provides possible solutions or a basic platform for life. Security has no distinction between rich or poor. Take time out. I believe serious frustration can lead to uncontrollable anger.

In my opinion children at an early age magnify their problems leading to the development of debilitating fears and loss of self-esteem, and once again the learning process encounters excess baggage like a magnet and develops the Curtain of Fear, real or imagined. Parents, help your children to develop a passion and belief that they can succeed and be happy in life. Teach them or more importantly show them how to develop relationships with their fellow members of the human race instead of competing and doing whatever it takes to succeed. Are we too driven without the human element? Remember, it's okay to be human.

In all senses of education, a child's first exposure to life and consequences is the family. It is the basis for a child's interaction with society, the key point in a child's academic success. It is the challenge of the parents to provide their children with the basic foundation so that each child may have a key to his or her future. Parents, you must take time out and sincerely join your child in meaningful dialogue, because after all, it is their future well-being at stake. We must also teach them how to make qualified decisions in life and to have a keener idea of their consequences. Which brings me to the computer: why not use this valuable tool to help children in this ever-changing world? How can we achieve this? Perhaps a software program can be created to allow children to make decisions and tabulate the results in a real-life setting. This allows the child ownership as well as the consequences of their choices. We already have their interest in the computer. But remember the computer is not smart; it is a tool. Let us expand it in a constructive way. I believe this will have a lasting effect on their ability to make meaningful life-long decisions based on solid data and not emotion. Of course we never make emotional decisions as adults. Right? I believe this exercise of decision-making can have a life-long effect and possibly help our children through the emotional curtain of fear. And allow your children to make mistakes, for the world is not perfect, and neither are we. If your child builds this idea that they cannot lose or trip on the boulders in life, watch out. Real-life decisions and the ending consequences are to be shown in light of truth. Remember your children are your responsibility seven days a week, twenty-four hours a day. You should embrace this responsibility for the well-being of your children now. Love, respect and truth.

Chapter II:
The Birth of the Gang

Kudos to the mother, father or other authority figure in the family when trouble comes to their door and they face it down. Make it perfectly clear that your children belong to a family. I believe we may have lost generations already. It is high time to recognize these types of situations and immediately implement a corrective action plan before your child brings death home. The family must and will survive.

We must form a true partnership with education and business: not what just looks good but that which is most positively productive for the better common good. We need to adequately prepare our children to be contributing members of the world. Self-esteem, focus, birth of the gang, anger, frustration—we always comes back to these situations in life. That is something or someone replacing the role of the family. How do you say thanks to grandparents raising a family twice? We must recognize that some basic elements are missing in the world today.

In my opinion we are not building enough prisons if we do not take action to keep the family together. Wow. Parents and families, take a hard look at the following and stop pointing fingers. The health and well-being of our society should be everyone's priority. Murder, drugs, and grand theft are but a few: why would a family protect a child who partakes in violent actions? Why would a family protect? Because it is all they have, and when there is no family, they fill the void with a gang. Ladies and gentlemen, it is far too late to start asking questions when the family member brings death home. Society blames instead of taking a sincere look at what is happening around them. But we have to take the time out to look. As always, there are consequences for actions. The first ultimate responsibility belongs to the parents. I don't believe there is another stronger force or influence in achieving inner confidence, peace and self- worth of a child than the parent. And above all, there is the special bond between the mother and child. Think about your own relationship or address the feelings you currently feel. Aren't they powerful? All children should also take a moment out of your life and visit with that parent as they become older.

Parents need to be aware of the present challenges in life. We should be teaching our children to turn negatives into positives, and to handle real life situations in a positive way, not to point fingers and backtrack. Always tell your children the truth do not play games. Remember, they will play games when they become adults, or sooner. Remember, children will make mistakes and they must know it's not the end of the world; and keep your words soft. Parents, it's ok to be human. I did not set a very good example at a few sports functions in my career. But I was always man enough, or more accurately, I was mature enough to return to the field and apologize for my frustrating, immature actions. This was the right course of action. We are all human; we just need to take time out and keep in mind that we are setting an example for our children— perhaps one they may carry for a lifetime. Saying you are sorry is not a sign of weakness but of character. Once again remember you are a driving force in your child's life. With every knock there is opportunity. Do not miss the chance for a positive resolution.

Chapter III:
Origins of Excess Baggage

How long can this excess baggage be held before the storm? It is evident that there are many storms dormant in each and every one of us—that means society, too. The whole human race should help find the key to unlock their child's untapped energy in a positive way whereby each child may learn to interact in a constructive way so that all our children may realize the fruits of their efforts. Pre-school is definitely a great idea that helped two of my children succeed early on. My middle and youngest child attended pre-school and are doing quite well. Once again not all children come to school ready to learn. How many parents appropriately prepare their young children for this major change in their life? I am of the firm opinion that an early start is a major component in the maturity of the child. Let us gather information from a nationwide survey based on solid statistical data to support a corrective action plan now. That data must be real life. I believe the results of the study will yield some positive points to act on, and I mean act on now. That also depends upon process of evaluation being universal.

Just as in the topic of testing, the playing field in dealing with children is also uneven. Cultural diversity must be factored in. I believe generations of welfare must be addressed. In some families welfare is a way of life. At the end of a school year during my tenure in education, I noticed a leather jacket and a pair of tennis shoes in a student's locker. I told the student not to forget his personal items. "Your parents sacrificed to purchase them for you," I said.

The student's response was, "No way, the government purchased them. I will just get new ones."

I was not irritated by this. I merely felt the system merely failed to address the basic question of self-esteem vs. value. To help a family out temporarily in a time of crises is one thing. But to continue with welfare will damage the individual's self-worth, making him reliant on money freely given.

This brings me to training and skill development. People judge without taking the time to understand that folks trying to survive will not take the time to evaluate where they are in life, and more importantly, how they can change their lifestyle to become contributing members of the human race. What about the school administrator who says, "What, do you want to be a gas station owner?" What about the other school official who equates being fat to being a child of African descent? Are we truly in tune with the complex cultural diversity of a society? Or are we engaging in dialogue or action that makes a school district look good? We should be addressing the issues that will enhance the child's ability to succeed and be a contributing member of society.

Yes, there are inalienable differences. Teaching in New Orleans taught me a number of lessons I will never forget. Once before school the first day I was there, a student broke my heart by telling me, "Why would you help? You're white."

I said, "Please don't hold that against me because I care about each and every one of you."

She responded, "You are different."

Let me share with you my first day of class. I said, "Will you people please be seated?" The students all stood up and left the classroom.

In my solitude the intercom in my room activated and the principal said these words, "Mr. Pettee, will you please come to the office."

I was stunned as I worked my way down the hall to the principal's office. As I opened the door to the office area all my students were standing with the principal as I looked at him and he said, "Mr. Pettee, did you say will you people please be seated?"

You could feel the tension. I responded, "Yes, sir, I did."

The students then said, "See, we told you he was a racist."

I responded, "Wait, I am people, you are people; are we not all part of the human race?"

They said, "Oh, ok, he's from the North. Lets go back to class."

At that time I received a most valuable lesson in life, one I will never forget. It was not a pejorative statement nor one to offend anyone. I was merely asking students to please be seated so that we could start class. The message was sent honestly but it was received and interpreted as a negative statement. How many times does this situation take place in this world? All members of society are different and should be recognized for their strengths and talents. What about the intelligent child who comes from a broken family? The world is made up of individuals who are different and possess special talents and come from different socio-economic backgrounds and make up a major portion of the equation. How do you reach them? Remember, your method of teaching is extremely important and can have a profound lifelong effect on your students

Abusive situations are another major contributor to a child's baggage. However, we can acknowledge them, take responsibility for them, and move on with life. Do not sit and procrastinate; do not hold on to past transgressions but move forward. Anger held from childhood needs to be addressed NOW. The adults who harbor anger, frustration, and that lack of a healthy self-image can and will allow those problems to rise to the surface again later on in life, probably as the children mature into adulthood. Where did the murderer come from? Where did the problem child come from? Conflict resolution, repressed feelings: a student in trouble. The parent states it's the school's problem. When the parent is made aware of a challenge, how do they respond? Put the child in jail or take a belt out for discipline. Can this action result from lack of knowledge or years of repressed feelings? Maybe it is the way they were treated as a child and feel this action is appropriate because that's the way the way they were treated. Can this represent the lack of self-worth and frustration that drive our children into a complete breakdown with totally uncontrollable anger and violence or simply not attending school?

Maybe it is time to gather data. How can we take start today? And what formal training has the parent taken to help the child navigate through life? Let's talk about the gifted child from a family of privilege. Do you think for a moment that low self-esteem and frustration affects only the economically disadvantaged? I tell you I believe that some children of successful folks have self-esteem problems. After all, their talents and emotions may and will vary. Not all students have the same intellectual capacity, nor do all families have unlimited resources. Parents of children not of privilege may not have the extra time and money to insure their children an opportunity to succeed.

While teaching in a vocational pilot program in the South, we were asked to prepare a dinner. We prepared a fine one with all the students. Let me share with you a powerful moment. The students were asked to come out at the end of the function, so I assembled the students and said, "Go out, be proud, and enjoy the moment. I am proud of each and every one of you."

Their response was heartwarming, "Mr. Dave, we're not going out unless you go with us."

I proudly accompanied the students. I picked up the microphone and asked the students to tell us their name and their home school. When I put the microphone to one student, the words would not come out. The joy, the pride and excitement was too much. I believe these types of accomplishments and recognition must be a way of life. This success was accomplished after a rocky start at the beginning of the school year. I had told these very same students the ill-fated statement "Will you people please be seated?" We are now a truly successful team communicating openly.

Remember, there are inalienable differences across the country between cultures, and that means everyone. It is imperative that we recognize these differences and work on our individual strengths. Although the dinner was great I was told the biscuits were hard as a brick. Never bake biscuits until the day of the event. I responded that I was from the North. I too received an ovation. Remember that God, family, education, listening, learning and teamwork help us on our journey through life. By the way, when in the South and cooking, they have a passion for good food and if you make red beans, make sure you have plenty of gravy.

Parents, again, be ever vigilant. Children may build up fears by watching your actions and listening to your words. A parent without knowing can project their fears and insecurities. Parents, accept your children with unconditional regard or love and remember you are the first teacher that your children encounter. If you have more than one child, make sure you share with them that each one is special and you genuinely love each one. Situations are going arise that are very serious.

When I was an assistant principal, a young student came to me and said she was contemplating suicide because she has no one to talk to. Think about that statement and the loneliness the student must feel, possibly the ultimate feeling of despair. I believe many students are dealing with loneliness and unable to deal with the overwhelming challenges life presents daily, especially peer pressure. That is why our children need parents to be there to communicate and help them reach their full potential and be happy. How will they handle life challenges? Could it be alone? When you drive down the road and observe somebody weaving or stopping without signaling, a number of thoughts come to mind. Or if you pull in front of someone in a parking lot, watch their anger elevate. Has a child learned at an early age the only way to fit in or resolve a conflict is to fight? The challenge will be to channel this energy into peaceful resolution. If it's not there, how can they begin to understand their feelings? And as your child matures, your relationship must reflect trust, understanding, love, and nurturing. Make sure that you clearly spell out the ground rules, and more importantly that your child understands the consequences of his or her decisions.

Let's look at children in trouble or in gangs: where do you think they come from? And when I hear parents say the schools aren't fulfilling their responsibility, my question is, are the parents taking time to talk with their children and help them report to school ready to learn? Is this the case? I think not.In the belief that schools are an integral part of society, the family forms the foundation. I believe some parents are under the impression that when they drop their children off at school, their responsibility is over. Your children are your responsibility first, 24 hours a day, 7 days a week, 365 days a year. These children need a firm foundation with security, a nurturing environment, and formal education if they are to be contributing members of society. What are some of the attributes of rejection and low self-esteem? Drinking, drugs, fighting, uncontrollable anger and frustration all contribute to disaster. Have we lost our basic values? Or have they been replaced with greed and selfishness? What about teaching children to compete at an early age instead of teaching them to get along? Get involved with school boards and your local government, and see how your ideas are received. Help your children to learn and interact at an early age, not to compete. Forget grades in the primary grades; teaching them to get along and interact in a positive, human way should be paramount.

While driving home, I was shocked to hear this story on the radio. The report started out, "...A women partially clothed, lying in a parking lot, while bystanders walked by and offered no assistance. At a nearby building, someone stated, 'Look, it's a peep show.'" Finally a person so disgusted with everyone's response took the time to call the local police. Folks, please keep in mind that this person is also part of the human race.

Chapter IV:
Testing in Schools

What affects the way we teach? Whose values are reflected in the material given? Remember always that we are accepting someone else's values or judgment calls in the world of education. I recently read in an article where I live that IQ tests are higher, although the proficiency tests are lower. Is that paradoxical in the world of education? Perhaps we should explore the construction of the tests. Could the design of the test possibly be faulty? I therefore ask the following question:

Question 1. Who constructs a test?

What criteria will be used with a universal approach? Who gathers the statistical data?

What does the testing of students accomplish today? Did you know there are inalienable differences between the states as they relate to culture, environment and the way each family lives? Goals in education can be universal, but careful consideration should be given to the procedure or the methodology we use to make sure our children are truly learning. We assume that the proficiency tests gather sound statistical data from all walks of life, all countries of the globe represented in the United States, and among all age groups. The second question I would ask is:

Question 2. What is done with the results of these tests?

Can one test accurately tabulate what a student learns or does not learn? I think not. It should be used to find out where deficiencies exist so that we may focus on the deficiencies and their resolution or adjust our teaching methods. Is the goal of tests possibly to encourage competition? Competition will come about naturally. How can a class learn together if at an early age they do whatever it takes to become number one? Why not teach children to greet and learn about each country's culture validated by native tongues? Understanding and unity may be factored in. All folks of good will want peace—let's embrace the principles of peace and begin the process now for all countries. Let's begin by the understanding and the sincere airing of pain among separation and all it entails. Remember, this is not the time to make demands. It is a time to air hidden or public feelings. After this meeting, which may take an extended period of time, can we zero in on the specifics? We must take time to get to know one another and nations or there will be a cloudy vision. Let us tear down the barriers to world peace now. Are we missing the challenge of helping young folks gain as much knowledge as possible and failing to promote the team concept and benefits of working together? Are we doing what's right or are we acting on what looks good in the school system today? The honor student brings prestige to a school, but where do the other students fit in? Are they worth nothing more than a seat in a classroom? We should shift focus to the marginal achiever working to capacity. Which brings me to the belief that the IQ test at an early age cannot and will not accurately predict intelligence or potential with such little data and time to gather knowledge. What about all the variables stated above? We need to keep in mind that we are branding a child for life. I believe we have lost generations of children already. How can I say that? Look around.

It is therefore possible that the creation of aptitude testing is faulty in principle and practice. Are we so focused on optimal testing that we have overlooked the method by which we convey data and the method by which children and adults learn and retain knowledge? It may be more meaningful to address teaching methods first. So where is the true measuring stick? I believe that there is a tremendous amount of ambiguity in some tests. But I think it is the Neanderthal who responds with the statement if they know the material: it should not be a problem. The child should be put at ease and the test should be progressive. How many folks out there are excited about taking a test? There's your answer. There are other contributing factors. What about the child with low self-esteem, upset stomach, anxiety, broken home? What about the child that could not have breakfast? What different procedure will be used for them? We must pinpoint deficiencies. Hence all these factors must be addressed to formulate and devise an appropriate plan of action. Let's go back to the statement "Take out a piece of paper; no, take out a blank piece of paper." Sound familiar? My third question:

Question 3. Could you tell your son that if he does not do well on this test he will not be admitted to whatever institution of higher learning he would like to attend?

Can this be constructive? I think not. It is destructive. We have also set up a system where it is possible to pay to take a class that teaches us how to take a test. Shouldn't the information conveyed in a classroom be sufficient? It is my opinion that this faulty process and the pursuit of knowledge did not accumulate over night—or did it? Are we constantly trying to look good or are we truly in tune with the well-being of the child and his or her academic success? But more importantly, we have not helped our children develop critical thinking skills. Empowerment or responsibility—aren't we making life long decisions daily? I wonder if these decisions are made with emotion or based on survival. And I wonder if this faulty decision-making happens to a lot of folks many times in a day. Can children make qualified decisions in the world market without proper persuasion and a full understanding of the consequences? Then we should be teaching our children constructive critical thinking skills in school so that they may attend school and receive an education.

Years ago one of the managers I worked with pulled out a book for a situation I questioned him on. I said, "What are you reading?" I will never forget his response: he said he memorized his books while in school. In my mind he wasted four years of his life. I believe an education will give you guidelines or a foundation and more critical thinking skills so that they may arrive at a logical solution based on solid statistical data. Perhaps it is time for revision, and ultimately devising a new approach.

Chapter V:
Teaching and the Curtain of Fear

Teaching is the message sent/received in the true light of its meaning, helping children see the light at the end of the tunnel. My question is, are some children even in the tunnel? I think many are not. Teaching is a real challenge in today's world. When there is a breakdown in the family structure, maybe it has an adverse effect on the perceived self-worth of the student. What is wrong with a child not of privilege who does not yield accurate results when being tested? I am certain that their self-esteem has been injured somewhere along the way and possibly to a point that they feel they may not succeed at all. I was one of those children. I did not mature until much later in my life. I was full of emotion and unable to see the entire picture. Do you think that some children feel they cannot compete on the same playing field as I did? I certainly think so. Children have so much unleashed energy that sometimes their power struggle is almost palpable. The key might be how to channel that energy in a constructive way, and that key lies in the hand of the teacher.

Keep in mind you are dealing with a diverse group of individuals with an equally complex social economic backgrounds. To say that one method of teaching will address the needs of all students, I believe, is in error. In my opinion, teaching in this day and age requires a great deal of collaboration with fellow teachers on a regular basis.

I also believe that some teachers also develop a great deal of frustration with the administrator who is not in the classroom on a daily basis and may not be open to new ideas. I am not saying that administrators are not managing; I am merely stating my opinion that education today presents new challenges in reaching all students. The dedicated teacher today has a lot of challenges in the classroom. Are we being faced with another negative challenge whereby administrative leaders could be taking the lesser path of resistance? Or is it simply being out of tune with what's happening in the classroom? Or worse yet, maybe some are too timid to make appropriate tough decisions after collecting pertinent statistical data. Maybe the question should be about what is right and not what looks good. Are the monies received by the local school districts utilized in the best interest of the children? I wonder if there are any incentives for schools to save money, or do they spend and spend? What happens to the money at the end of each fiscal year? Is the planning appropriate? So many questions to be answered; are school districts ready to answer them? If you had to find answers to these questions, would you know whom to ask?

This apathy in administration was evident when I heard another statement in the face of a tragedy: "I guess I am in charge." Could they be out of touch with what's happening today and therefore unable to address current operational and educational issues or provide meaningful direction in a challenging new time? What about the well-educated school person who asks an employee without a degree, "What, do you want to be a gas station owner?" I believe teachers have the ability to teach and that all administrations should allow them to do so. It is my belief that you cannot teach from the office. It is important for the teacher to establish a professional relationship and understanding with each student and his or her parents.

Sometimes the teacher must be creative as well as innovative to capture the moment to create an environment whereby the key is found to unlock the energy that may be dormant, or channel it when in full-swing in each child. The ultimate goal is to harness that energy in a positive direction. Maybe collaborative workshops should happen many times a year. This needs to be addressed. Teaching is a dedicated life profession and not for those who do possess a passion to empower and lead our children. They must maintain a passion for what they accomplish on a daily basis. Keep in mind teacher appreciation is paramount, for many hours are accrued outside the classroom. Don't ever assume for a minute that a teacher has it made having the summer off: the preparation and energy that goes with the job exceeds the classroom time. Let your teacher know you sincerely appreciate their efforts, for it is a labor of love. Money is not synonymous with education. It is understanding the child, sifting through the excess baggage, and devising an appropriate way to reach all children.

I understand that everyone must deal with pressure, teachers as well as students. I feel this situation can create a curtain of fear, however, a curtain of fear that each child must pass through alone. What about peer pressure? Did you ever see a marginal child get recognition for working to capacity and not achieving an A? I don't believe all children have the same capacity to read and to study, to learn and to test, which all contribute to a child's potential curtain of fear. Maybe we should recognize the child for his or her individual strengths, not weaknesses.

When I was a child, test-taking used to scare me. One day in college, my instructor told everyone to take out a pen and a piece of paper. I was so nervous and scared that I returned my paper in class without any answers and a zero written on it. My test paper was later returned to me with a note stating that she would like to speak with me after class. At the meeting she asked what had happened. I responded that I had blacked out. I don't think I could even remember my name. She said that I participated in class and could not understand why I put a zero without any answers. She then said, "Let's go over the test verbally." In doing so I answered all the questions perfectly. She said that in the future she would administer the test orally. I wonder how many folks out there have had similar experiences.

Now let's look at the physically impaired. UCP states, "Look at me, not my shell." When I worked at the Special Olympics with disabled children, I just wanted to do everything for them. They just wanted to be like other children. Let them be independent and succeed on their own as a whole person. The emotional makeup of each child should be paramount. Don't start building anxiety at an early age. Our children have enough stress going from the security of the home to a different structured challenge or setting in life, such as school. School is a life-altering experience and life- long journey for all children; let's make it a positive one. We must also keep in mind not every child is perfect, or should we say, no one on earth is perfect. Do not think for a minute that children don't feel that pressure to be perfect. Each child is special. My dear sister has a little girl with Downs Syndrome. She is so beautiful and completely aware of her surroundings. She sings, dances and roller skates better than I do. I remember when she would deliberately fall after skating with absolutely no trouble at all. Then it became apparent that she was falling simply because everyone else was. Her motor skills are excellent and she started school equipped with more love and self- esteem than most children. She has been loved and nurtured by both parents and the extended family. She is simply happy. The smile on her face is very special smile for a very special child.

There is a great amount of diversity in the approach to teaching, but the universal theme is that all children have baggage and challenges. All types of baggage and challenges can be met and defeated with positive reinforcement, focusing on their strengths, and allowing them to grow into their own path regardless of class, race, or ability.

Chapter VI:
Business and Schools

Never forget that school is big business and it is conducted daily. May I make another bold statement? I believe they need to communicate on the same playing field as very few are. How can we strengthen this communication process? Quite frankly, I believe the following action must happen first from a practical standpoint: all parts of the human race, and I mean the global human race, must sit down with a complete overview of each other's position. From the business sector, they must prepare all their thoughts, needs, requirements, and how they will make this program work. All parties to the human race must agree as to the assessment and projected success of this unprecedented action. I believe that we have already lost part of the population to drugs, murder, hate, low self-esteem, suicide, and broken families. Just look around. There is not a minute to waste. School systems are an integral part of success for humanity as well as business. All parties must embrace the philosophy that the end result will allow children and adults to be contributing members of society. Success and happiness will go along with the necessary skills to do so. This must be done without prejudice or bias. That means no exclusions due to age, color, origin, gender or physical ability. After all, in this day and age we have the means to reasonably accommodate the physically handicapped. The proper statement should clearly reflect the fact that all persons in the human race have some limitations. This should not and will not affect the person's inalienable right to attain a skill and to live a fulfilling, happy life. After all, everyone belongs to the human race.

I am not bashing the system, although I believe improvement is also a life-long challenge. I don't adhere to the statement "if it isn't broken, don't fix it." Once again, whatever happened to gathering statistical data? That may be logical and yield a practical solution. This is an example of the Peter Principal whereby the person is elevated to his or her highest level of incompetence.

When a company moves out of an area and opens a new shop in a different state or country, do they begin to exploit the area with substandard wages? Do you think these companies are operating with that philosophy before they moved or do you think this is a move to generate profitability? How much profit is enough? How much is reasonable? What happened to the line of communication and trust and, above all, working together? I wonder what happened to that trust. I have never seen a CEO perform every job in the plant. If you listen to some of them on the news, you would think they did. What happened to the CEO who thanks the worker no matter what his or her job may be? With all the big business scandals in the news, I believe that something is wrong. Schools are under a similar amount of fire with failing test scores. The voucher institution may be innovative and necessary. What is the real question? Could it be accountability?

While in negotiations with the unions, I was asked a question by the business representative about medical coverage. I responded, stating that I did not know but I would find out. At that moment, the business rep leaned over and acknowledged me, saying, "Okay, next item; when negotiating, do it honestly."

Let me share another disturbing situation I encountered in the field of education. While concerned about the work environment and my goal of creating a positive atmosphere that allowed each individual to reach his or her potential, a fellow administrator approached me and told me, "Stop trying to be liked. You cannot create a perfect workplace." I am very suspect of a "well-educated" administrator making that type of statement. I truly wonder about that person's self esteem and management style. Would you feel secure working with an individual making that type of statement? Why can't we all create a positive environment whereby each individual can contribute fully and work together in harmony? I don't believe we can motivate anyone directly, but I am of the firm opinion we can create an environment whereby each employee can realize his or her potential. My response is simple: maybe if everyone would move out of their comfort zone and drop their ego and self-proclaimed superiority complex, maybe, just maybe mind you, we will all do a better job and move forward together.

Education reform is like the tree that has fallen in the village, impairing the basic operation of the village. The tree was far too heavy to be removed by one person, although not an impossible task for the entire village to achieve if each member could firmly grab a limb and move the tree together. Then the tree could be relocated to an area that will not impair the flow and well-being of the village. It may only be accomplished with all folks working as one, moving in a predetermined direction. It is too bad that the tree of education has not moved in any direction. Many individuals, however, have attempted and subsequently failed.

Chapter VII:
Origins of Anxiety and Responsibility

Anxiety is a major non-productive, destructive impediment affecting the way we teach. With all its medical repercussions, we should stop and look at worry and its value with a careful eye. We would certainly stop if we knew the damage it actually caused us physically and mentally. It is a learned behavior. What is its origin? It stems from every walk and way of life. It comes from everywhere. It would be a great feat to eliminate forever, but we must analyze it first to make sure that we are not operating and making value decisions in life based upon anxiety. It is appropriate and necessary to focus on current issues in life based on statistical sound data, not worry or fear. Not one issue from the past can be changed with all your worry today. Start today planning and living. For instance, you must be aware of the child's background so that you may develop an IIAP (Individual Improvement Action Plan), not respond to a child's problems and worry with emotion and shortsighted action. It has a direct impact on the well-being of the child. All children carry excess baggage vs. an emotional decision that has as a negative impact on the way we live life and interact with our partners in the human race. It is like the student who is distraught over not having a parent to talk to. He/she worries about what

37

will happen to him/her, worries about being different. These feelings may result in destructive behavior or possibly a cry for help.

What about the parents of a child who engaged in criminal activity at school who arrived at our scheduled parent meeting, and the first question from the father was, "Just what did my child do?" I pulled out a list of items and gave it to the parents to read. The father responded, "Well, put him in jail or call the police."

My response was, "Aren't we talking about the well-being of your child?" At that moment the tone changed and the student received help. Years later while visiting the school, the student stood, walked to the back of the class where I was observing, and gave me a hug. The well-being of that young person was preserved and the necessary help was administered. We all have the consummate responsibility to care for the well-being of all our children and interact with one another in a positive way. We are all integral parts of the human race, and it is never too late to bridge the gap in our differences and promote our strengths as we all strive to be contributing members of society. This simply means creating a global awareness.

Everyone can criticize and point fingers. History should be analyzed for future action. After gathering data, an appropriate plan of action should be developed to increase global awareness. Sounds fairly easy? Not so simple, however. The evolution of the world and what happened yesterday may not be the key today. Let me share my belief that today we are all experiencing a great deal of frustration, and the end result of that condition will have an adverse effect on the quality of life. We cannot change history no matter how hard we try. What we can do is try to avoid the pitfalls of today and not retrace the footprints of the past. If history teaches, why are we not listening? Or more importantly, ask yourself what have you done today to make this world a better place in which to live. If your answer is nothing, here is a wonderful opportunity to plan to do so. Please take time out and share your thoughts with your family. Remember, the family is the basis for society.

There are so many dangers out there for your children as they grow. Drugs and alcohol have become increasingly dangerous substances in these times. That is a constant worry that will wear away your entire sanity. The solution is communication from day one. I have kept such communication with my children open.

One day my son came up to me looking rather upset. He said, "Some kids wanted me to smoke with them, Dad. I told them that I do not smoke pot and I do not hang out with kids that do." He looked up at me and said, "Dad, I made the right decision."

I said, "Son, I am proud of you. Yes, you made the right choice." That very same son wanted an earring. Is that so terrible? Smoking pot is. I always pray that my children always have that trust in me. But one day you will have to let go. This answer is much simpler than waiting breathlessly to see them grow into responsible adults.

Parents, just keep the lines of communication open. You will ultimately help your child navigate through a maze of danger as they grow. What about the father who wonders why his son does not play football simply because other parents have children who play? This situation happened to an acquaintance of mine. He stated that he asked his son, "Are you going to play football?" The son responded that it took up a lot of time, pain and energy that he would rather spend on something else. Does this mean there is something wrong with this teenager? Absolutely not. Parents should realize that not all children necessarily want to play football, or sports, or musical instruments, or even follow in their fathers' footprints. Could this mean the parents are trying to impose their will on their children instead of allowing them to make a decision as to how they mold their own high school life? If you take wood against the grain, you may take away its natural beauty. The same goes for your children. Successful children may not follow in their parents' footsteps, so parents, take the time to listen. Nurture and develop the child's own image of self-worth. I always wondered why privileged children did not succeed when they are given successful businesses without the heartache. Why in God's name aren't they successful? They do not share their parents' vision, for one. Why? Maybe because that child is frustrated because they have lived in their parents' shadow all their lives. Allow your child to grow and make some decisions as to what they would like to do in the pursuit of happiness and achievement. I wonder if there is some ego involved. If the father is a successful businessman (a professional going to another profession and vice versa) or other professional, the child should have the opportunity to choose. But the question might be whether or not the child can make that decision in the marketplace without proper persuasive guidance and formal education. It is our consummate responsibility to guide them and help them navigate through life.

Chapter VIII:
Formal Education and Skill Development

Today in American society, the importance of a traditional four-year degree is given much prominence. That same thought should include a trade school which may not be a four-year degree. Parents, going into a trade that doesn't involve years of higher education does not mean that the child is less of a person. Understand that I am telling you true education is on the road *to* the pursuit of happiness. Think about that statement on the road to happiness. This goes back to the belief that all persons in the human race possess a great array of talents, and during life you will accumulate a lot of skills. The child needs to know from you that everything is okay. Do not be concerned or worry about what your so-called friends say. Do what's right for your child and focus on their strengths. Not all students will accomplish a four-year program. However, they must have a skill, and that skill makes them no less or better than a person with a four-year degree. Once again, your child needs to know it is all right.

I never thought I could succeed. I was a victim of a curtain of uncertainty, the curtain of fear—debilitating fear that people would not like me and that I would fail. I lacked a sense of belonging. Are we not all part of the human race? Society does not always include everyone, but we as members of that society can include all people. Folks, not all people will like you for whatever random reason, and you will not like everyone you come in contact with. That it is okay because no one is perfect. What's important is the fact that we can all live in this world in harmony. This begins with a sincere respect—respect for all individuals regardless of their origin. Think for a moment what a dull place this would be if we were all the same, trite but true. Children are often labeled as a "problem child" or the "class clown." Has teacher burnout taken its toll?

Let me share some experiences of overwhelming egos and assumed power whereby a person honestly believes that they are legends, even if only in their own minds. I questioned a professional once, asking him directly why he was such an *******. He then smiled. I took one look at that smile and told him, "You enjoy being an *******."

He actually smiled a bit more broadly and said, "Yes." Think about that for a moment. He enjoys making everyone miserable. People like that are out there. Are you going to give that type of person control over you? I think not. If a person states "You made me angry," ask them how that is possible. You allowed yourself to be mad. If you accuse somebody else of making you angry or upset, you are in for a rough time. Do not give them power over you.

A doctor I once asked why he was so unapproachable for such an educated and talented man responded that he did not want to have a relationship with his patients; it affected his surgical skills. What? It was almost unbelievable, and later when I thanked him, he said, "Bull****." Wow. I thought it was odd that a well-educated person would make that kind of statement, keeping in mind they have control over our medical well-being. I do not fault all doctors, but there are a few that make me stop and think. Maybe they should take the time to hug a pile of gold. I am sure some received a feeling, cold or other. Folks, it is okay to have a heart. It occurred to me that it was time to make a number of changes in my life. Maybe that particular doctor should look into the mirror and face the fact that he is not God and put his ego in check. I have been exposed to some real winners in that particular profession. I have since made some changes in the type of medical care I now receive. Recently I thanked a doctor for the excellent care he provided. His response was a Christian one. Thanks to all good doctors who genuinely care about the patients and their well-beings, although this is only my opinion. Thanks again, Dr. Stephen Habusta and Dr. S. Hejeebou for your professional care.

Always allow your child to have a passion for what he/she would like to do. Don't box your children in, do not let anybody else place their value on top of your children's, and above all, do not project your feelings as to what they may or may not do. Offer suggestions.

It is like a cooking class. A student said to me, "Mr. Dave, I have burnt the food product."

I asked him, "Did you burn it good? And do you know what caused it to burn?"

He looked at me and responded from the heart.

Look at that situation carefully. First and paramount is the fact that the student had the strength to talk with me. Where else can a child learn and take responsibility for his/her actions? I felt great that I had gained his trust. It is so important to be aware of his/her lack of success.

Most importantly, there are challenges in life. When you look at the situation, look at the positive side and not the negative. Understand what went wrong so you can avoid or deal with that challenge in the future. Remember that you do not want the student to give up because of possible failure. Keep the lines of communication open. Nobody in the human race will make correct decisions all the time. What's important is the fact that you did attempt a feat and moved out of that comfort zone. It is okay not to achieve success all the time, but to never try is not okay. I ask you how many children don't challenge the world? That is sad. Whatever your skill may be, do it with pride and strive to be the very best in that field. Have a passion for what you do. If you are forcing your children into careers that they do not have a passion for, please stop. You may make poor statements that have a life-long effect.

Chapter IX:
Parenting 101

I will never forget the moment when my son Daniel was born, and the intense joy of being a father. I consider myself to be very strong and together. In this case, however, they had to put me in a wheelchair before the nurse would give me my son. I have three sons, and all three are very special. May we all remember that unconditional regard; our children are an ultimate expression of our love. I am sure the liquid coming from my eyes was due to the light and the uncontrollable perspiration all over, and the constant shaking was due to the heat. My pale color was probably due to the lack of eating breakfast. I have no idea as to why the nurse gave me juice. Do the fathers out there remember this moment as well? Whenever times get tough, remember the very first time you laid eyes on your children.

Take time out to listen, parents. Weigh your words when you are with your children. When my wife and I were first married, we did not have a great deal of money. Even so, my children watched and picked up everything. This was evident when my one son said, "Dad, when I grow up I want to be a cash register because they get all the money."

Or when your injured child is taken to the hospital, watch

your words. When my son injured myself and required a tetanus shot, I said that it would not hurt. When I needed a shot later on in life because I had stepped on a nail, he leaned over, looked me in the eye while placing his little hand on my shoulder as I was sitting in a wheelchair and said, "Dad, don't worry. It will not hurt." The reaction of the medical staff was precious.

Will parents possess the necessary skills to dissociate the situation? Or how are parents going to respond when emotions hit the curtain? Goal-setting as a family may be the answer. Simply take time out and ask your children, "How did your day go?" and "What did you learn today?" Stay involved, parents, and use caution in responding to your children's concerns. You do not want to void their decision or their critical decision-making process. Let them develop in independent thinking. Remain calm and provide positive direction. Keep the lines of communication open or you may give your children reason not to communicate.

You must also help them statistically. Don't overreact. It is my belief that you are the in a position to guide them and allow them to make independent decisions by communicating as a family unit. I believe that your position may help them on their quest to becoming a contributing member of society. Who knows, later on you may not otherwise be involved in their life if you don't involve yourself now. They will not make time for you if you do not make the time for them.

I would like to share a spring break vacation with you. For two weeks we toured the coast of Florida, from Daytona Beach to Shark Tooth's Cove to Disneyland. At the end of some of the days we walked on the beach and looked for sharks' teeth. We ate at various seafood restaurants and had a great time. On the way back we were sitting in the camper and I had my arms around my boys. I said, "Hey guys, did you have a great time in

Florida?"

They looked up at me and said, "Dad, it was great just being with you." Think about that statement. It did not cost a lot of money but it certainly made me take another look at my life and my priorities.

Sports have been a large part of my involvement in my children's lives. Baseball, football, basketball or soccer games were a delight for my wife Jeannine and I. I have always appreciated the smile and pride when they saw me arrive. Mom was always there, a special mom who is my beloved wife and best friend. My sons were always proud to see us but always asked respectfully that we not shout, "I love you, man" at the end of a play or home run. I am proud of my sons, and they are not ashamed to tell me that they love me, too. I firmly believe real men hug their sons. Being a parent and family member means hugging your sons and daughters, if only because it has been a while. Married couples' communication can simply mean a touch, a hug, a kiss, kind words. Let me share a moment while in church with my wife: I put my arm around her. She did not come closer, so, concerned, I asked her if she was upset with me, and she said, "No, honey, I just can't see."

I must say I have really made some questionable statements in my life when involving myself in my sons' lives. My children have always had exceptional teachers over the years, but one day I made a real blunder. Facetiously, I told my son to ask his teacher what kind of broom she rode to school on. The next day my son Daniel asked his teacher that unforgettable question: "Mrs. ********, my dad wanted to know what type of broom you ride to school on."

Smiling, she said, "Tell your dad it's a turbo model and it's in the closet."

I cannot express the emotion I had with myself as I took

ownership for my words. She was a special teacher with a sense of humor, to say the least. Then came the news: "Dad, here is the schedule for the parent-teacher meetings."

Let me share another story about a special fishing outing I had with my son Dave. We were fishing on the bayou at Plaqemans Parish in Louisiana when my son suddenly dropped his fishing pole in the boat and ran behind my back. I said, "Son, you have a good one."

His response: "Dad, that's not a fish." (The power of listening to your children.) I grabbed the pole wondering what made him so scared and started reeling it in. Lo and behold, it was not a fish but a rather large stingray.

We laughed and I said, "You are so right, son." Nevertheless, he did not venture too far from my side for the rest of the day. Now my son is 30 and we still chuckle about it. The power you have as a parent is very strong because your children always look to you for support; and I was there for them.

Evenings when the children had nightmares also exemplify this. My son Daniel used to have nightmares about Freddy Kruger. One night he came to my wife and my room crying. He told us very seriously, "Dad, Freddy's gonna get me."

I told him, very honestly and simply, "You tell Freddy I'm gonna kick his butt if he bothers you again." I don't recall another incident where Dan had a nightmare about that ugly fellow.

Communication with my son and positive direction is vital. The other day I received a call from my son at work stating he was ready to quit his job. He went on to explain the challenges.

I responded, "Son, did you talk with the manager?" and he responded, "No."

I said, "In life there will be challenges, and you can not just quit all the time."

He said, "Okay, Dad, I will talk with him." Twenty minutes later he called all excited, saying all was well.

I responded, "Son, I am proud of you."

It is a rare feeling of relief when parents strive their whole lives to impart values in their children and they are rewarded by something they did. My son found a purse while working for a local grocery store and promptly turned it in. When the customer arrived to pick it up she could not believe it. She rewarded my son with a five-dollar bill. I am proud of all my sons, and the values my wife and I would try to impart have hopefully survived. It must be a constant practice in life and business to exercise these values at all times.

How can this be carried over in life without undo turmoil? Let me share with you my basic view about God, family, life, business and the pursuit of happiness. It is the family that is the basis for society. This carries over into life as well. Working harmoniously together for the same common goals in life sounds rather like a good family, doesn't it? Although once again the worker is expected to share the vision of the employer no matter what the employee's background. Do you think that a child will be receptive to learning when he or she is trying to survive? Once again, is it good for an educator to stand up and say you need a four-year education to be successful in life? Could you tell your children they need to successfully complete four years of chores to be successful in life? I am sure that any person will be receptive or embrace the true meaning of the message sent or possess a comprehensive understanding of thriving in a positive work environment. That is the kind of environment that is ideal for children to grow up in.

Finally, always treat your children equally. Once, my son Andrew was experiencing a challenge and his statement to me was "You went to school for Dan, but you will not go for me."

I said, "Tomorrow we will speak with your teacher." We agreed on a time and presented our case to a most caring teacher. I must tell you that we were focused and merely stated the facts, and the results were positive.

Keep in mind that as your children grow and mature, you must be ever vigilant and listen. It will help them immensely. How many of you have been frustrated and said to the child, "I am going to straighten this teacher up." Keep in mind that your child may be listening. You must always present yourself professionally in a calm, cool, statistical manner. Do not attack and enter into non-constructive dialogue. Don't let things get out of hand.

Chapter X:
Wealth and Lifestyles

Do you think for a minute that folks do not want to elevate to a better lifestyle whereby they may realize the fruits of their labor? I am of the firm opinion they do, but they do not know how to or the fear of the unknown prevents them. I do not necessarily mean simply moving out of a comfort zone. I am talking about debilitating fear of the unknown, of uncharted waters. If their parents never experienced security or achieved little success, then how can they share or direct their children? Look at the emotion, or the curtain of fear, or personal self-perceived inadequacy. It all comes back to self-esteem and our self-worth. It is the very essence of the individual. I am of the opinion that the child is worth this meaningful yet radical corrective action plan. May this study for helping children to help society begin as soon as possible. It starts with involving the parents and the family.

Could a child contemplate suicide, terminating his own life due to the fact that he feels he has no one to talk to, especially in the early teen age group, when he is undergoing tremendous hormonal changes? At this point, children are not sure what is really happening to them, and they are unsure about with whom they can speak about these matters. It is ultimately the parents' responsibility. Sometimes the parents may not see the signals. They may even be unsure about what to do about them. I firmly believe that you must be ever vigilant and take the time to communicate with your children.

First, parents, do not box your children in. The parents must lay the ground rules and the consequences for violating them. I believe that parents cannot lay down all ground rules at the same time. The basics first, and the rest must rely on honest, open discussion with a fusion of trust and real-life experiences as well as maturity on both sides. I did not mature until late in life and faced a number of frustrating moments. No one is happy all the time, not even me.

I understand that everyone must deal with pressure, especially children. I feel this situation creates a curtain of fear that each child must pass through alone. What about the peer pressure? Did you ever see a marginal child get recognition for working to capacity yet not achieving an A? I don't believe all children have the same capacity to read, study, learn and test. Maybe we should recognize the child for his or her individual strengths, not weaknesses.

Have you talked openly with your children? Have you looked at what their strengths are and together given some direction or thought as to what the children would like to do or not like to do? Start planning early if you do not have any idea as to where you are going and how you are going to get there. Now this sounds like a basic plan to the child not of privilege or their parents, but will a parent possess these types of parenting skills when they are trying to provide the basic necessities of life? What is really sad is the family that is not aware of the help and direction that is necessary and readily available to elevate them from poverty. Can the child internalize this and feel like he/she is a lesser individual? Yes. I believe this situation propagates the emotions of fear, anger, and violence to ultimate despair, and the feeling that they cannot compete and be successful and happy. The last situation you want to occur is the child holding this frustration inside, because that fact, coupled with being boxed in, provides fuel to an already explosive situation. It is no surprise to me that the child moves out of that boxed-in situation with a seemingly uncontrollable fury full of myriad emotions. I tell you that this type of destructive behavior happens daily, and the parent responds to the situation in anger, elevating the situation to its most destructive mode. The results forever break down the family structure, ultimately destroying the family. If you believe, as I do, that the basis of society is family, don't we want to strive to avoid that end? A lot of parents will respond in anger to these emotions after a day of survival and economic duress, propagating this situation to heightened levels. Why can we not address this now before it elevates to that new level? Are children exhibiting this violent behavior as a direct result of the breakdown in the family structure? Could they have learned this action from seeing the parent react in this manner and consider anger as a way of resolution? I would say yes. Remember: Parents provide powerful direction by *listening*. Be careful not to project your fears onto your children's already frenzied minds. Just being there is sending a powerful message that you simply care.

Societal needs have changed dramatically over the years. Are we asking the right questions? Goals and learner outcome are fine. It is the procedure that we must implement or design that will yield positive results that are necessary. Procedure method is not business as usual if we are going to give all children a chance or opportunity to succeed in this constantly challenging world we all live in. What is success? Money? Gold? If you had the opportunity to lie down on a bed of gold,

I bet the feeling would never compare to a hug. God, family love, positive self-esteem, education and friendship are forever. When gold is gone, its legacy is gone. What is lasting and warm are love, peace and family. Ask yourself what is success. Redefine your goals and values today. As you reflect, ask yourself what is truly important. What have you accomplished today to make this world a better place in which to live and prosper? I'll give you a hint: making lots of money doesn't count.

Sometimes I wonder if someone is compromising values, or more importantly, if society is trying to make the abnormal normal. Is the quest for wealth justification to destroy the human spirit? Is wealth to be shared or is philanthropy a way of easing the mind before death? A retired executive stroked out in retirement, stating, "I would have lived differently." Society is crying for change. Why vouchers today in schools? What is happening with our schools today? We are members of an educated society that can't publicly admit and properly educate students without sending them to private schools. When you discuss the pedagogical elements of society, I would bet the average person would not understand what the heck that meant. Pedagogical means the educational elements of a school district. Speaking in terms that all may understand would be a good start. Do not use the above phrase. I was told I was no one because I did not have a B.A. degree. I was focused and attained it with pride. I was not a child of privilege. While in my forty-something year, I earned my Masters in education. I had very caring, helpful instructors. During my program I had a lot of support from my family: my wife, my mother and an advisor who helped me on my journey to attain my B.A. and finish graduate school. I would not have been successful without their help. A heartfelt thank you goes out to Dr. Daniel Merritt for all his professional help.

Take the time to look around. Listen to the news. Is greed taking over human rights? A company grants bonuses to executives and then files for bankruptcy. Keep in mind the corporation waits until the checks are deposited and cleared at the bank. I also heard a heart-warming story, where a school system and a caring business won a title together. In my opinion this shows a true partnership between education and business. Congratulations to the students and teachers. It is beautiful and so much fun. They worked hard and it paid off. No idea is without merit. In my opinion success is imminent with a true partnership between education and business. Implementing a project of this magnitude and achieving this type of success should be explored. The statements from the students indicate a sense of accomplishment and pride. This was a true partnership with a collaborative approach. Certainly these are the types of articles that should be focused on.

Chapter XI:
In Times of Crisis

In our family we have a zero tolerance to drugs. However, when I was young I asked my father to share a beer. He did. Let me share an interesting scenario with you. I first entered the service and completed boot camp, and upon arriving at my first duty station was in the process of opening my door with the key that was on the chain around my neck. Another airman asked me what I was going to be doing tonight. I said that I was real tired after unpacking and will probably unwind a little and then go to sleep. His response: "Come on, let's go get drunk." I will never forget how he said that. I said, "What, didn't you ever have a drink with your dad?" He said, "Never. My dad would have killed me." That is something he would never do at home. I share a beer with my sons just like my father shared with me. There is no mystery about it for them, so hence there is no desire to abuse it.

Let me share with you an incident concerning my brother. This is an example of family values necessary when times are tough. Here is an incident where my mother was worried about me and related her feelings to my brother Denis. I had received word that my brother Denis would come visit me where I was stationed in Texas. Boot camp was a challenging time for me at Lackland Air Force Base. I have to say that for a seventeen-year-old (nearly eighteen) away from home for the first time, I needed someone to talk to. Therefore, my mother called my brother Denis, who was already in the Air Force, to share some of my feelings. My brother stopped by the chow hall to say hello. As basic recruits, we were not allowed to sit down before a higher rank. After the D.I. observed me sitting, he said, "Get up. You don't sit before a higher ranking."

My brother responded, "It's ok, Sarge. He is my brother."

I certainly will never forget his visit as a family member and military man. My younger brother Joe was also a part of my family's lives as my children grew up. When my son injured his arm once playing sports, he said to call his uncle first. Joe, who is a very sharp and experienced nurse, after a careful analysis told my son that he would need to see the doctor. My son responded with a question about what should we do. My brother went on to explain. When my son arrived at the doctor's office, he said, "This is what you need to do because my uncle Joe said so." The doctor smiled and said okay.

Another dangerous milestone in my life was once again during my tenure in the Air Force. I was on watch when a person in my platoon approached me with a knife and forced me to the ground. I watched my life flash by in a second. I asked calmly after he told me he would kill me, "Do you need the knife to be a man?" Thank God he said no and threw the knife. I never had words with this young man, although he was full of hate and anger. Today I do not hate that young man. Although I could have indulged in self-pity and allowed that hate to be part of my life. I chose one of peace and forgiveness. I have matured a lot in life and grown beyond that.

What children are learning ties into how well we are dealing with challenges in life. Socio-economic influences are major part of a child's learning process. For example, when a student was asked to read from the class textbook, the student responded that he didn't feel well. Not to embarrass the student in front of his fellow classmates, I went to the next student, who responded in the same manner. I stopped and asked, "What is going on?"

The students responded, "We cannot read." Here is a potentially damaging situation that needs to be addressed in a positive way on an individual basis. I started to realize the challenges to devise a plan to help these students be successful, helping them gain the education to deal with challenging times ahead.

Did you also hear about the controversy involving mentioning God in our daily lives? What a major crisis of faith we have in this country. It is a shame that some folks feel that it is not appropriate to reference His name in school, work, or government. The statement that our country was built on the belief that "in God we trust" must cause some people to feel that the universe and human race were based solely on molecules bumping together. I feel sometimes that our rights and freedoms are being infringed upon. Take abortion for instance. It is taking an unborn child's life. Everyone speaks about the rights of the mother and so on. Who protects the life of the unborn child who has an implied right to life? I believe that child has an implied right to life at conception. The folks here today in this world are lucky because they had the right to be here. Are you not surprised that you had a right to life? Repercussions of this chill me to the bone. What a lack of respect for life. Are we now in a throw-away society where children are in the way? There are some major changes in the values of life and responsibility that must be made now.

Chapter XII:
Moving Out of My Comfort Zone

I moved from my comfort zone and enrolled in the Culinary Institute of America in 1977. I had a lot of experience and some basic culinary skills, so I started gathering statistical data to form a plan. I registered for CIA that year and took the chance. I would like to share a positive experience I encountered while attending the CIA. Early on in my first year, I jumped in and started flipping eggs in front of the class. Yes, I thought I was pretty good. The chef instructor took me aside and stated, "Let us show you our way so that you will understand the proper techniques and procedures."

I returned to earth. I said I appreciated the opportunity to attend the Culinary Institute and that I would maintain an open mind as to the fine professional direction it provides. You must have an open mind to learn skills for there are many variations. Once you have a firm foundation, your opportunities are endless. Did you ever learn anything by listening to yourself?

I currently have three degrees with honors. Yes, I moved from my comfort zone and focused on each degree, including the associates from CIA. I did attend the graduation ceremony and I am glad I did. My wife said, "Honey, you should go." I recommend it for all graduates.

When I was seriously injured, lying on my bed in tears and really feeling sorry for myself, my wife leaned over and hugged me and said, "Honey, everything will be okay." Once again, I sure needed to hear that statement. I knew from that point on everything would be okay. My wife is the brightest, most loving and beautiful driving force in my life. While feeling sorry for myself and magnifying my challenges, she will say to just take each day at a time. She helped me understand this theme. I am sure no one else engages in this type of self-pity. Such is the power of a good partner whom I asked to marry on the second date. She responded, "No, you are crazy." After 32 years I am still crazy about her. She is not American, and this sends a powerful message that two countries can live together in the same home and experience peace, love and happiness. My wife is a proud Canadian, and I am proud of her, and so are my sons. I also have great in-laws whom I love dearly.

One younger person my wife works with said, "You and your husband never have disagreements."

She responded, "We have some good ones." They were shocked at the response. The message here is to please communicate, and if you genuinely love that person, do you not want them to be happy? Remember, no one must be right or wrong; in winning, you could be losing. As you talk about a number of sensitive issues, be considerate and listen. No one is a puppet. Let go and move on. Some folks do hold on, and this anger creates an array of problems. Therefore communicate and live in harmony; if not, what are you holding on to? Not one situation in the past can be changed with worry, no matter how hard you allow yourself to indulge.

After I had gotten my Masters from the University of Toledo, I did not want to walk at the ceremony. I thought I was too old to walk with all those young students. My comfort zone was tightening its grip. It was my wife, bless her soul, that helped me jump that hurdle. All grads, no matter what their age, should attend their graduation ceremony. They've earned it. This is also a great example for your children. Above all else, you did it for yourself. Pass that courage along. My mother provided strength to a dear friend. My mother has attained her Masters after the untimely death of my father, raised my sisters and brothers, and always focused on education and family values. It was a challenge and a success story. My mother passed her courage on to a dear friend, Bob, who is well into his fifties. He stated the following: "Your mother took my by the white-knuckled hand and helped me in my pursuit of a B.A. in business." Once again, thanks, Mom. He currently has only a few more classes to go and will also receive his B.A. He was an infantryman in Vietnam who has now walked through that emotional curtain and out of that comfort zone twice and is succeeding. Congrats, Bob.

I was a spirited one after my four years were up in the military, and my father was very ill. I took him to lunch to thank him for the strength and drive he had helped me develop, as well as for the hard-working example. He had also imparted the sincere belief that you can and will make it, no matter what. Do not give up, and should you fall, get up, dust off and proceed. When I shared all this with my dad, he started to cry. He also told me he loved me and that he did the best he could. The tears and the inner peace cannot be described. My message is one of peace. Before you make a decision in life to carry out any expression of hate and anger, look at all data. It will most likely be someone else's loved one as well as another human being. So before making an emotional decision that you will live with for the rest of your life, make sure you are at peace with your family and loved ones. Do not forget good friends, either. Before one passes, please make peace.

Chapter XIII:
Dealing with Frustration with the System

How well will you deal with another challenge in life? Have you ever experienced a number of challenges when you are already on overload? I am sure you say "Let's take a look at the situation and explore possible solutions in a rational statistic manner" if you've read all the way thus far. Correct. Can true anger and total frustration lead you to believe that you are not going to succeed? You noticed that I did not say fail. Failure should not be in your vocabulary. Nobody fails in life unless they choose to. You must believe that you can succeed. What is so sad is the person who has all the necessary tools to be a major contributor to the well-being of society and yet does nothing. That means they must move their comfort zone and they chose not to. Society is full of opportunities. Hopefully, we have the wisdom to recognize them, and more importantly, how we can play a major roll by taking a pro-active position and becoming a key player. These practical ideas possess global application. No matter what your geographic area, you are still an integral part of the world community and a vital component of the human race.

My family is an international one. For many years I have been an example that two nations can live in harmony under one roof. What is important here is the fact that we have always had the lines of communication open. Over the years she has always given expert advice and support. When I was seriously ill and very discouraged, she leaned over, hugged me, and said, "We will make it together and all will be okay." I sure needed to hear that. And wouldn't you know it, at that moment I knew all would be okay. Or the moment when I came home complaining and my wife looked at me and said, "Honey, you are unhappy with me." You could have knocked me over with a feather. In marriage it is imperative that you listen because we can send negative messages without realizing it.

I responded to my wife and best friend of thirty-two years, "I am just having a bad day." What if she would have held it in? Can you see: each partner must have the freedom to express themselves openly. If the relationship is rocky due to poor communication, just imagine the results.

Parents, let me share with you cultural understanding. I made a well-seasoned gumbo and had it ready to serve upon the arrival of our family members and dear friends. I preceded to dish up the gumbo. At the end of the meal, I waited impatiently for the results to come in. I said, "Mr. Earl, how was the gumbo?"

His response, "It was good, but in this area we place the rice in the bowl first, sprinkle it with gumbo file, and finally ladle the gumbo over it." I said okay. The next time he just looked up and smiled. I now have a greater sensitivity and understanding of the words cultural diversity. With a background in food and the creativity of my loving sister, I would like to share a basic combination with a powerful message in life, using the ever-loved chocolate cookie with all its vital components. Let's begin with flour, sugar, eggs, chocolate chips, butter flavoring, and so on. And from an educational standpoint you must:

1. Read the recipe; English
2. Weigh the ingredients; math
3. Follow a number of procedures; scientific method
4. Bake it at a special temperature; chemistry.
5. TLC.

Could this be the perfect example of how all parts of the human race can go together in harmony? It certainly would not be a whole cookie without all the basic essentials, though. Why can't we all go together in harmony, appreciating each other's natural strengths and beauty? It is our focus to devise a method, because if it works for a cookie, with human input...

Chapter XIV:
Sales

When you thank family, friends, business associates, and strangers, I am not sure you are aware of the impact and power of those two words.

In business after receiving the order I said, "Thank you."

The customer looked at me stunned; she paused and said, "No, thank you. You are different."

I said, "I truly appreciate the opportunity and value your business."

Don't forget the thank you. Also, I never learned a thing listening to myself speak, but you can learn a great deal listening to your customer. Do you like to hear someone that likes to hear him or herself speak? When you are in the audience, write down the words you cannot understand. Hopefully that pompous speaker will identify the type of crowd he/she is to address. It is the ultimate responsibility of the speaker to draft a speech that can be clearly understood by all. After all, he who receives the value of the message ultimately places a value on the time spent listening. Ever wonder why folks get bored? They may have lost the thought being shared. I believe speakers must be innovative, knowledgeable as to core content, and present it in such a way that all folks can understand the premise. At any time you might invite feedback or make yourself available at a later date. People know when you are sincere. If it is worth saying, do it in such a way that the targeted crowd can receive, digest and use it to improve the quality of life. Caring messages are to be shared for the health and well-being of all folks in the human race. And it is everyone's responsibility. My legacy will be that I was a loving husband, father and family member. I never aspired to be the wealthiest, although I would like to be remembered as a person who contributed to the well-being of this world.

While making a sales call, I was there to sell my services. I broke one of my golden rules: never go into any account without two business cards; above all, never take your accounts for granted. As I approached the service counter, a new face appeared in front of me. I greeted the customer and offered my business card. There was only one problem: my business cards were in the car. I said, "I will get a business card from my car." I gracefully smiled and said I will be right back. I walked calmly to the door but when the door closed behind me, I ran over the hill and along the parking lot to my car. I grabbed a number of business cards and ran over the hill to the entrance and stopped after a few moments to regain my composure. I professionally walked up to the counter with my cards and secured the order.

After the sale, I started to walk out when the station manager said, "Dave, have you got a minute?" He had a great big smile on his face. He said, "We saw a blur running past our window." I shared with him that I had forgotten my business cards. He said, "You really hustle." We all laughed together. When on your job, do the very best job that you are capable of and you will be rewarded when you hustle, if it's not the reward you may expect. It sends a positive message that you care. It is service and a total commitment to the customer.

Why do people respond to you in a negative manner? Did you ever look at your approach? I once listened patiently to my employee as he explained how this customer's employee responded to him. I said, "I would like to go with you."

He said, "Well, this employee will come flying around the corner with a real attitude."

"Okay, now I know I need to go with you."

The situation happened just as he said it would. While standing on a dock, he came through the door with a bandanna on. As he approached the back of the truck, he stopped and placed the pallet on the truck with care. My response was, "Wow, what a professional job." He almost fell off his horse. I said, "You are one of the best tow motor drivers I have seen." And then he proceeded to tell me about his job. We had opened the line of communication. We all laughed as we started to leave when someone parked in front of the truck. Well, we are not perfect, although a sense of humor and a positive attitude helps. Try looking for the positive in everyone. It works. Leave your gloves, clubs and attitude at home and grab your sense of humor. Remember, not everyone has a perfect nature. A sense of humor goes a long way. Watch the face of a truck driver when you say "Have you got your happy face on today?" I crack myself up sometimes. It is nice to see a smiling face instead of a long one. You must have a sense of humor in life and never hold on too tight. Have faith and inner peace will come.

Let me share another situation. When I was a manager in a restaurant, one of our waitresses came up to me crying. I said, "What's the matter? Things are not that bad."

Although she assured me that they were, she went on to say, "Don't go out there."

I said, "Wait a minute. Let's go together and resolve the

situation."

Upon arriving at the table, the customer laid into me for about ten minutes. I received the absolute worst straight-A chewing I ever received. When I thought she was done, I said that I was sorry. She proceeded to give me another tongue-lashing that rates high on the list. When I thought she was done, I said again that I was sorry. Finally she said, "Stop saying you are sorry." I was thinking to myself that was sorry I came out here. Finally her husband told her that that was enough. He then proceeded to tell me the construction of her new home was not going well. I wished her a better day.

Chapter XV:
In Closing

This book has helped me deal with a great level of frustration. Over the years, I have asked myself a number of difficult questions: how did this world evolve into its current situation is one of the big ones. I am merely stating that there are answers, and the first step is taking the time out to recognize them and resolve them as a society. Not one person or political party can correct our current state of affairs, nor is there a quick fix. It evolved over many years of neglect and greed. The political system, no matter how imperfect it may be, can still provide valuable input provided it is developed in a bi-partisan way in unison with a true partnership with schools, businesses and the human race.

Are we asking the right questions to insure our future? Stop pointing the finger. Can nations sit and break bread together? I believe it's time to let the past go and start living and acting as a true member of the human race no matter what your national origin may be. This world is for all who embrace freedom, love, and the pursuit of happiness. Look around and ask yourself what you have accomplished today to create peace and harmony. One might start by responding without anger and prejudice and extend the sign of peace. There is no way to change the past, so let go and begin to live a happy, full life. Embrace the challenges of life. Reach deep into your self while maintaining a healthy vision with a formal education. There will be sacrifices, but the prize is worth the efforts. After all, education is truly a lifetime journey. One needs the knowledge to adapt to the challenges life presents. It seems to me that we are walking around oblivious and totally insensitive to the human race. Today, we don't even interact on a positive note. Let the change begin.

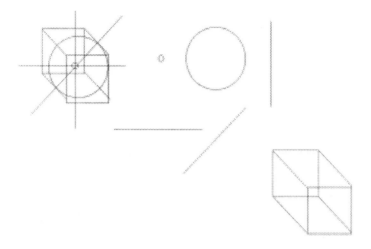

Where all congruent lines in the cube connect to one point in the exact center of the sphere through a Cartesian plane, at this point is where we, the world, need to come together in peace. At this point, all cultures and countries are connected for good or for ill.

Printed in the United States
66584LVS00002B/1